ABANDONED CALIFORNIA

THE SALTON SEA

ANDY WILLINGER

AMERICA THROUGH TIME

For Ericka

America Through Time is an imprint of Sutton Publishing Inc
www.through-time.com
office@through-time.com

First published 2021
Reprinted 2025

ISBN 978-1-63499-299-2

Typeset in Trade Gothic 10pt on 15pt
Printed and bound in England

CONTENTS

Acknowledgments **4**

Introduction **5**

1 Bombay Beach **9**

2 The North Shore **25**

3 Desert Shores **35**

4 Rancho La Playa **45**

5 Salton Sea Beach **51**

6 The Southeast Corner **59**

7 The Outskirts **70**

8 Salton Sea Naval Base **75**

9 Salton City **86**

Bibliography **94**

About the Author **96**

ACKNOWLEDGMENTS

Special thanks to Dr. Ericka Hofmeyer, Doris Robbins, Kurt Willinger, Doris Willinger, Jeremy Willinger, Matthew Willinger, Katie Willinger, Dana Stein Willinger, Michael Tingoli, Lucy Hofmeyer Lancaster, Helena Hofmeyer Lancaster, Fiona Hofmeyer Lancaster, Norman Hofmeyer, Jill and Wayne Nash, Scott Schaffer, Mark Warren, Ron Cukier, Todd Christensen, Kevin Lynch, Richard Misrach, Kim Stringfellow, and Dr. Jordan Perzik.

INTRODUCTION

In October 2019, supervisors in Imperial County, California, declared a public health emergency due to extreme air pollution at the Salton Sea, the state's largest inland body of water. The water levels there have been rapidly receding, exposing a dried-out lakebed laden with contaminants from industrial chemicals and military experimentation. Cadmium, selenium, arsenic, and other toxins are poisoning humans and animals as they breathe this ultra-fine dust. Winds are pushing up to 100 tons of toxic dust airborne every day, turning the region's existing asthma crisis towards disaster. Although the immediate area is sparsely populated, almost 1 million people in the Coachella and Imperial Valleys and beyond are directly affected. The nearby agricultural industry, which provides the majority of the winter produce in the United States, is also in jeopardy, mostly from airborne salt. The Imperial County emergency declaration sounds an alarm that immediate action is necessary, effectively acting as a Hail Mary attempt to secure state and federal funds to help suppress toxic dust.

This looming health catastrophe was predicted, as much of the remaining replenishing source of the Salton Sea's water, farm runoff, was diverted ten months earlier. Due to a federal and state agreement, the water has been diverted to urban areas in the San Diego region. Although local officials were given fourteen years to prepare for the diversion, no productive action was taken to mitigate the predictable damage.

This implausible water relegation is just another cautionary fable in the storybook of what was once a desert paradise. It has been a long, slow slide from being a glamourous desert lake resort towards the Salton Sea's current sorry state, as fluctuating water levels and pollution have threatened wildlife and human habitability for over sixty years. Despite spending hundreds of millions of dollars and numerous failed, delayed, and mismanaged projects to "save" the Salton Sea, this disaster may finally have reached the boiling point.

It is heartbreaking to think how such an astonishingly beautiful place can fall victim to a man-made disaster, but man-made disaster has long been part of the Salton Sea's story. Some 35 miles southeast of Palm Springs, it was created by accident in 1905, when irrigation developers attempted to harness some of the Colorado river's water for burgeoning agricultural development in the Imperial Valley. Unusually heavy winter rains overwhelmed a poorly constructed headgate near Yuma, Arizona. They caused the full flow of the Colorado River to empty northward into the Salton Sink, an ancient, salty dry lake prehistorically known as Lake Cahuilla.

The unrestrained river flooded the entire Imperial Valley for two years, submerging homes, towns, and thousands of acres of farmland. The massive New Liverpool Salt Works, which mined over 700 tons of pure salt daily from the dry lake bed, was totally engulfed by the flood. Its railroad tracks and train cars, along with New Liverpool's headquarters and employee's homes in the town of Salton, California, are still submerged underwater. The breach was finally sealed in February 1907, after a team of nearly 2,000 people finally restored the Colorado's southern path, eventually emptying the river into the Sea of Cortez in Mexico.

As a result, a body of water with approximately 370-sq. miles in surface area had remained, becoming the largest body of water in the state of California. It was called the Salton Sea. Averaging 30 feet deep, The Salton Sea's water was about 50 feet deep at its lowest spot throughout much of the twentieth century. Its nadir is 277 feet below sea level, which is only 5 feet higher than Badwater Basin in Death Valley, the lowest spot in North America. The northern portion of the sea is in what is considered the Coachella Valley, with the southern portion in the Imperial Valley. Both are major agricultural production areas.

The Salton Sea became what is considered to be an endorheic basin, meaning that its waters do not empty into a river or ocean, but mostly equilibrate by evaporation. Since its surface is about 238 feet below sea level, there is no lower point nearby for it to drain into. It is also what disputably qualifies it to be considered a sea, instead of a lake.

From the onset, the Salton Sea exhibited extremely high salinity levels—even higher than the Pacific Ocean. Despite the salty water and intense summer heat, this large body of water in the middle of the Colorado desert soon became a recreational oasis. In the 1920s, boating enthusiasts, knowing that high salinity increases buoyancy, flocked to the sea, which became a center of innovation for hydroplane racing. Racers also took advantage of the low altitude, which made their engine's carburetors more efficient. In 1929, over 2,000 people watched five world speedboat records broken on what was disputably called the "fastest body of water in the world." The Salton Sea became a hotbed for speedboat racing, with dozens of world records set there.

By the early 1960s, the Salton City 500-Mile Championship Boat Race became one of the USA's largest and most prominent speedboat competitions, attracting racing teams from all over the world. The event would draw over 60,000 spectators lining the shore to view the exciting race.

The Salton Sea lies in an extremely tectonically active area. The entire eastern coast of the sea runs directly along the San Andreas Fault, with geothermal activity present in the southeastern corner. In that area, there are five small lava domes known as the Salton Buttes, with fields of mud pots bubbling away from volcanic activity. Nearby, there are eleven power plants converting geothermal steam from below the ground into electricity.

In 1950, the California Department of Fish and Game began stocking the Salton Sea with saltwater fish. Orangemouth Corvina, Tilapia, Silverside, Croaker, White Mullet, Bonefish, Sargo, and other varieties were harvested in San Felipe, Mexico, and introduced to the lake with the hope of luring anglers to the area. The resulting influx of sportfishing enthusiasts encouraged the rapid development of a sizable tourism and boating industry.

Throughout the 1950s and '60s, the Salton Sea became a desert playground for the rich, the famous, and the everyday adventurer. Double the size of Lake Tahoe, the warm waters enticed water-skiing enthusiasts and became a major tourist destination in California. Beach towns such as Salton City, Desert Shores, Bombay Beach, and Salton Sea Beach sprung up to welcome millions of visitors every year. Noted architect Albert Frey designed the North Shore Beach and Yacht Club, which was the largest marina in Southern California when built in 1959. Frank Sinatra, Jerry Lewis, The Beach Boys, the Marx Brothers, and other top celebrities routinely came out from Los Angeles, 175 miles away, to luxuriously frolic in the sun at this desert hotspot.

The glory days at the Salton Sea would not last forever. By the 1970s, the water levels began to fluctuate greatly, flooding shorelines and damaging structures. Since the Salton Sea's main replenishing source of water is from agricultural runoff streams, the nitrates and phosphates from fertilizers increased salinity, heightened bacteria levels, and caused widespread algae blooms. These issues resulted in decreased oxygen in the water, causing many of the fish to die. In 1976 and 1977, massive tropical storms ravaged the region and severely damaged a great number of the resorts and marinas. This devastation caused the entire Salton Sea area to plummet into a lingering economic downturn. Its tourism industry would never recover.

Many of the residents of the seaside towns would eventually sell or abandon their homes and businesses, threatened by unpredictable water levels and its pervasive, unpleasant odor. The foul stench is caused by bacteria consuming the algae blooms, further exacerbated by the intense desert heat. As the condition worsened, the fish population died off in greater numbers, with their dried-out carcasses littering the Salton Sea's shores. In 1999, 7.4 million fish died at the Salton Sea in a single, extremely hot day. Many of the once-sandy beaches around the shrinking lake are now heavily coated with granularized fish bones.

The Salton Sea also has a massive bird population, with over 400 different avian species nesting there. It is a major stop in what's known as the Pacific Flyway, a route for migrating birds from Canada to Mexico and in between. The U.S. Fish and Wildlife Service maintains and protects a complex of waterfowl and wildlife refuges in the southeast corner, many of which are named after former entertainer and congressman Sonny Bono, who was an ardent supporter of the rejuvenation of the Salton Sea. This area has long been a major destination for ardent bird-watchers. Unfortunately, a growing number of the birds visiting the lake fatally contract avian botulism from the infected fish on which they feed.

The water level of the Salton Sea has decreased about 10 feet in the past twenty years, which has resulted in some shorelines being shifted hundreds of feet away from where they used to be. The sea continues to get about 3 percent saltier each year. Salinity levels have climbed from fifty parts per thousand in 2010 to sixty-seven parts per thousand in 2019. It has become almost twice as salty as the Pacific Ocean, which averages about thirty-five parts per thousand. More salinity means more fish and bird deaths, as well as greater jeopardy for the area's massive farming industry.

For the most part, these once glorious, vibrant, seaside towns have been reduced to bleak, desolate wastelands. They are sites of an epic man-made disaster caused by greed, apathy, and negligence. The fragile ruins of the Salton Sea's structures and vehicles are quietly disintegrating in the toxic dust and broiling sun. Surrounded by the sublime and capacious vistas of the Colorado desert and haunted by the spirits of their past, they can be viewed as fascinating monuments of humankind's complicated and tenuous relationship with nature.

1

BOMBAY BEACH

There is probably no town more iconic of the Salton Sea than Bombay Beach. Located in the center of the sea's eastern shore, Bombay Beach was once a prime destination for tourism and a bustling community of people mainly residing in upscale trailers and motor homes. It featured a marina, boat launches, restaurants, and numerous businesses to support anglers. Situated at 223 feet below sea level, it still has the lowest altitude of any residential community in the United States.

As such, Bombay Beach was repeatedly ravaged by catastrophic flooding in the 1970s and '80s. Fluctuating water levels caused by uncontrolled farm runoff and the winds and flooding from two giant storms caused substantial damage. The downgraded versions of Hurricane Kathleen in 1976, and then Hurricane Doreen in 1977, submerged Bombay Beach in water, then embedded nearly everything in mud and salt. A great number of the town's residents were forced to abandon their homes. A giant soil berm was constructed west of 5th Street to protect the surviving buildings, but the distance to potential employment, toxic air, and foul odor from the contaminated sea have scared away all but the most impoverished or cantankerous residents. According to a 2017 ACS census survey, there are only 341 residents left residing in Bombay Beach.

The shoreline beyond the berm has an otherworldly quality, covered with crushed fish bones amid skeleton-like foundation pilings and remnants of abandoned structures and vehicles. More than any other Salton Sea town, Bombay Beach has endured a degree of post-apocalyptic tourism in recent years, with visitors expressly coming to view the remnants of this devastated town. Many of the ruins have been defaced by graffiti artists with smartphones ready to immortalize their handiwork on social media.

In 2016, a group of international socialites formed the Bombay Beach Biennale, an art festival featuring permanent and temporary sculptures and performances.

While the festival has drawn visitors (and funds) to the community, many of the installations can be considered nothing more than art colonialism, effectively exploiting the devastation and mocking the poverty and desperation of the remaining citizens of the Salton Sea.

Embedded Motor Home. Bombay Beach. 2010

Delivery Van. Bombay Beach. 2005

Embedded Trailer and Chair. Bombay Beach. 2005

Embedded Trailer. Bombay Beach. 2010

Dredge Crane. Bombay Beach. 2012

Marina Ruins. Bombay Beach. 2010

Straw Hat. Bombay Beach. 2016

Dead Fish. Bombay Beach. 2010

Forsaken Skiff. Bombay Beach. 2013

Green House. Bombay Beach. 2014

Andy, Green House. Bombay Beach. 2011

Green House TV. Bombay Beach. 2014

Stripped to the Bone. Bombay Beach. 2010

Red House Skeleton. Bombay Beach. 2012

Four Ladies. Bombay Beach. 2011

Inferno Shack. Bombay Beach. 2011

Sears TV. Bombay Beach. 2005

Blue Shoe Pile. Bombay Beach. 2012

Living Room, 5th Street. Bombay Beach. 2012

Barbie Skate. Bombay Beach. 2014

Crackle Hut. Bombay Beach. 2013

Record Player. Bombay Beach. 2013

Baby Shoe. Bombay Beach. 2014

The Boat. Bombay Beach. 2016

The Boat, Profile. Bombay Beach. 2016

Deflated Raft. Bombay Beach Marina. 2012

Crepuscular Pier. Bombay Beach Marina. 2015

Dusklight. Bombay Beach Marina. 2015

Sofa Sunset. Bombay Beach. 2016

2

THE NORTH SHORE

The northeastern quarter of the Salton Sea has a prominent and storied history. Developer Gus Eilers built the Salton Sea's first *bona fide* resort there in 1926, which he called Date Palm Beach. It became a worldwide mecca for hydroplane and speedboat racing from the late 1920s through much of the 1940s. The town's name was changed to Desert Beach in 1947, and its new Desert Beach Yacht Club held many prominent regattas. Renowned orchestra leader Guy Lombardo was also a major boat racing enthusiast who set a world water speed record there in 1948. By 1950, Desert Beach was decimated by rising waters and storm damage.

Shortly thereafter, the competitive boat-racing scene shifted slightly northward to a new development called North Shore. The North Shore Beach and Yacht Club was built in 1959 and designed by Palm Springs architectural darling Albert Frey in his desert modernist style. Billed as the largest marina in California, it quickly became a hotspot destination of Hollywood's elite in the '60s and early '70s. Frank Sinatra, Jerry Lewis, and the Marx Brothers all kept boats there. Once again, the complex was ravaged by storms and flooding in 1981 and fell into disuse. The main building was renovated in 2010 and is now used for community and private events. One of the original buildings next to the club was not part of the renovation and remains in ruins.

Desert Beach still exists, reinvented as a gated community of tidy manufactured homes on the higher ground east of the shore. The westerly coastal area has been known amongst locals as "Sunken City", as many of its original buildings had been underwater for decades. Since the water levels of the Salton Sea have been receding in recent years, many of the long-submerged ruins of the "Sunken City" of Desert Beach are now becoming visible above the waterline. The shoreline of this area is covered entirely by granularized fish bones.

Further south on Grapefruit Boulevard lies Corvina Beach and Corvina Estates, which was a sizable mobile home community right on the coast. It was a lively community that capitalized on the Salton Sea's great boating and fishing opportunities. Almost no trace of its former glory remains today.

Continuing down Route 111, the shrewd eye can spot a strange, black building on the inland side of the road. It is the remains of an equipment shed for the former Eagle Mountain Railroad. Owned by the Kaiser Steel Corporation, this privately owned railway was used to disperse its iron ore and refuse to the Southern Pacific Railroad from the Eagle Mountain mine near Joshua Tree National Park. The railway shut down completely in 1986, years after the mine ceased operations.

North Shore Bait Shop. 2019

Corvina Café. Corvina Estates. 2010

Bait Shop Sign. North Shore, CA. 2019

Left: Motel / Lots. North Shore, CA. 2019

Below: Toro Loco. North Shore, CA. 2019

Yellow Tile, Sunken City. Desert Beach. 2019

Sunken City Ruins. Desert Beach. 2019

Fish Bones, Sunken City. Desert Beach. 2019

Gratuitous Sunset. North Shore, CA. 2016

Inverted Boat. Corvina Estates. 2019

Collapsed Structure. Corvina Estates. 2019

Embedded Speedboat. Corvina Estates. 2019

Equipment Shed, Eagle Mountain Railroad. Ferrum, CA. 2019

Avoid. Eagle Mountain Railroad Shed, Ferrum, CA. 2019

Equipment Shed and Tracks, Eagle Mountain Railroad. Ferrum, CA. 2019

Debris. Eagle Mountain Railroad. Ferrum, CA. 2019

Merging Tracks. Eagle Mountain Railroad. Ferrum, CA. 2019

3

DESERT SHORES

The first significant residential community on the northwestern corner of the Salton Sea, off California Route 86, is Desert Shores, a town developed in the 1950s. Desert Shores was once a beautiful community with excellent access to boating, fishing, and recreation on the Salton Sea, but it has suffered from the area's common hazards. A well-designed marina gave the residents of 374 trailers the ability to moor their boat right in front of their homes on their own private dock. Desert Shores also became a major site for speedboat racing in the late '50s and early 1960s. The algae blooms, fluctuating water levels, tropical storm damage, and the "Salton Sea Stench" have made living there difficult, boat racing impractical, and tourism untenable.

Desert Shores featured an upscale shoreside mobile home development called Marina Mobile Estates. The adjoining clubhouse, known as the Desert Shores Yacht Club, had an impressive midcentury modern clubhouse with swimming pools and shuffleboard courts overlooking the marina. While a portion of the residential development remains, the once swanky clubhouse has now been entirely razed, with almost no trace of its existence remaining.

Despite the harsh conditions in the town, over 1,000 people still live in Desert Shores. The canals of the marina have mostly dried up, and the haunted detritus of abandoned residences and businesses are scattered throughout the area, especially around the shorelines. Even the fire station has now been abandoned.

Welcome. Desert Shores. 2019

Depleted Marina Channel. Desert Shores. 2019

Anchor House. Desert Shores. 2019

No Worries. Desert Shores. 2019

Pink Algae Bloom. Desert Shores Marina. 2015

Green Algae Bloom. Desert Shores Marina. 2016

Toy Truck. Desert Shores Marina. 2019

Exterior, Desert Shores Yacht Club. 2015

Interior, Desert Shores Yacht Club. 2015

Organ. Desert Shores Yacht Club. 2015

Fireplace, Desert Shores Yacht Club. 2015

Lover's Luau. Desert Shores Yacht Club. 2015

Jacuzzi, Desert Shores Yacht Club. 2015

Interior, Desert Shores Yacht Club. 2016

Fireplace, Desert Shores Yacht Club. 2016

Swimming Pool, Desert Shores Yacht Club. 2016

Dark Skies. Desert Shores Yacht Club. 2016

Firehouse. Desert Shores. 2019

4

RANCHO LA PLAYA

In between Desert Shores and Salton Sea Beach on California Route 86 lies an easily unnoticed area. A blue-and-white sign marks the development as "Rancho La Playa." This was formerly the site of Sundial Beach, a prominent speedboat racing spot in the 1950s. The beach featured excellent swimming, campgrounds, a boat launch, equipment rentals, and boat sales and repair. After fluctuating water levels hampered the usability of the beach in the mid-1960s, the area was repurposed as a Boy Scout camp, according to locals.

Ownership of the 152-acre property purportedly fell to a man named Leo Borunda, who called the development "Rancho La Playa." Borunda had spruced up the park-like, palm-laden complex to include a master residence, imported banana trees, a giant Grecian statue surrounded by an ornate swimming pool, a large concrete pond, and numerous outbuildings. The property was occasionally rented out for concerts, private events, and hosting an environmental group. Allegedly, Borunda had grand ambitions of building multiple homes and a conference center on the property, but those plans were never completed.

After Leo Bournda passed away in 2014, the property fell into neglect and has been vandalized repeatedly.

Gate. Rancho La Playa. 2019

Residence Porch. Rancho La Playa. 2019

Restroom and RV. Rancho La Playa. 2019

RV Driver's Seat. Rancho La Playa. 2019

Haze I. Rancho La Playa. 2019

Swimming Pool. Rancho La Playa. 2019

Winnebago. Rancho La Playa. 2019

Pond and Ramada. Rancho La Playa. 2019

Blue Sailboat. Rancho La Playa. 2019

Blinded. Office Trailer, Rancho La Playa. 2019

5

SALTON SEA BEACH

Further south from Desert Shores along California Route 86 lies the sleepy little town of Salton Sea Beach. Salton Sea Beach had a beautiful, expansive sandy shore designed for families to enjoy swimming, watersports, and fun in the sun. Much like the rest of the Salton Sea, fluctuating water levels wreaked havoc on the town, with only scattered remnants of the once glorious past still visible.

Today, the coastal area of Salton Sea Beach resembles a true apocalyptic disaster area. The shoreline has receded hundreds of feet eastward, and the sand is covered with granularized fish bones. The carcasses of freshly deceased fish continue to wash up every day. Numerous motels, restaurants, and residences have been abandoned, vandalized, and some have been set ablaze. The channels of the Salton Sea Beach Marina have almost completely dried up, with its clubhouse and tackle shop completely demolished. The implausible site of a 1970s vintage speedboat embedded nearly perpendicular in the soil eerily hints at the massive contradictions of what once was and what now has become of Salton Sea Beach.

Trailer and Dead Palms. Salton Sea Beach. 2016

Marina Entrance. Salton Sea Beach. 2015

Little Shack. Salton Sea Beach. 2019

The Palms Motel. Salton Sea Beach. 2019

Shoreline Timbers. Salton Sea Beach. 2009

Red Chair. Salton Sea Beach. 2009

Embedded Speedboat. Salton Sea Beach. 2015

Speedboat Gauges.
Salton Sea Beach. 2015

Zebra Trailer. Salton Sea Beach. 2019

Tires in Restaurant. Salton Sea Beach. 2017

Burned Trailer. Salton Sea Beach. 2019

Hope Has Left. Salton Sea Beach. 2015

Fish Head. Salton Sea Beach. 2013

Tire Lounge, Salton Sea Beach. 2015

6

THE SOUTHEAST CORNER

The southeastern corner of the Salton Sea has long been the most bucolic and undeveloped area of the Salton Sea. The farthest point away from Southern California's populated cities like Los Angeles, San Diego, and Palm Springs, it escaped the development and tourism booms that exploited much of this desert sea in the 1950s and '60s. As a result, much of the southeastern corner became a protected haven for wildlife. Aside from a few access points, the shoreline was never improved and was allowed to remain a marshy wetland area where migrating birds could nest and refuel on their Pacific Flyway route. This area, including the Sonny Bono Salton Sea Wildlife Refuge Complex just to the south, remains a major destination for bird watchers from all over the nation.

The town of Niland, on the Salton Sea's easternmost edge, was an agricultural hub in the Imperial Valley, with an impressive columned bank building, warehouses, and a connection to the Southern Pacific Railroad. Since its heyday, the town of Niland has suffered severe economic decline, and many of its buildings have been severely neglected or abandoned.

Niland had a well-developed boat ramp park that provided anglers and boating enthusiasts access to the Salton Sea, but the waters have receded so drastically that the ramp can no longer be used. Its shoreline has receded hundreds of yards, leaving a white, dusty playa replete with toxic chemicals.

Since the Salton Sea's eastern shoreline lies along the San Andreas Fault, the southeastern corner has an abundance of geothermal activity. In between some of the agricultural fields are active mud pots, bubbling away with volcanic venting. This area also includes what is known as the Salton Buttes, which are a group of five hills that are actually lava domes. They are named Mullet Island, North Red Hill, Obsidian Butte, Rock Hill, and South Red Hill. There are eleven power plants nearby to harness this geothermal energy from the ground, with clean energy developers clamoring to build more on the exposed lakebed.

East of Niland lies the site of a former U.S. Marine Corps base called Camp Dunlap. Defunct since the end of World War Two, the military razed the base in 1961, leaving little but the concrete slabs that its buildings were built on. Slowly, a group of squatters discovered the abandoned base site, building shacks and parking their RVs on the slabs. Now known as "Slab City," it has been developed into an informal ragtag community of misanthropes, artists, addicts, and the disenfranchised. Its residents are essentially camping in an anarchistic wilderness—with no water supply, no sewer system, no waste disposal, and no power source (although some locals have installed solar panels). Its nickname of being "The last free place in America" is not too far from the truth.

While Slab City is a ramshackle active community of over 150 residents, it is by far from abandoned. There are, however, many burnt-out and forsaken vehicles and some interesting ruins from the original military installation.

Rubble, Red Hill Marina. Calipatria, CA. 2019

Red Hill Marina. Calipatria, CA. 2013

Niland Boat Ramp Building. 2018

Boat Trailer. Niland Boat Ramp. 2018

Playa with Landlocked Dock. Niland, CA. 2019

Warehouse. Niland, CA. 2019

Warehouse Loading Dock. Niland, CA. 2019

Skylight. Niland Warehouse. 2019

Living Room, Niland Warehouse. 2019

Farmers Bank of Imperial Valley. Niland, CA. 2019

Plywood Pier. Niland, CA. 2013

Catamaran. Niland, CA. 2019

Abandoned Trailer. Niland, CA. 2019

Guard Shack. Slab City. 2019

Festooned Truck. Slab City. 2019

Burnt Bus. Slab City. 2019

Camp Dunlap Swimming Pool. Slab City. 2019

Blue and Orange House. Niland, CA. 2019

Bomb Tower. Frink, CA. 2014

7

THE OUTSKIRTS

There are several nearby areas that have been directly tied to both the Salton Sea's successes and its failures. To the north and west, the cities such as Coachella and Indio are part of the agrarian breadbasket whose irrigation runoff supplies water—uncontrolled, contaminated water to replenish the sea. As the fortunes of the Salton Sea have shifted, so have many of the nearby agricultural, industrial, and residential developments. A host of ruins, from the mundane to the peculiar, lie abandoned on the outskirts of the Salton Sea.

Palm Gate. Indio, CA. 2015

Alien Terrain. Indio, CA. 2015

Sailboat and Tires. Indio, CA. 2015

Red Foundation. Indio, CA. 2015

Irrigation Hoses. Indio, CA. 2015

Abandoned Warehouse. Indio, CA. 2015

Complex Foundation. One Hundred Palms, CA. 2019

Sloop. Coachella, CA. 2019

Irrigation Hoses with Palm Tree. Coachella, CA. 2019

8

SALTON SEA NAVAL BASE

About 10 miles south of Salton City lies the remains of the Salton Sea Naval Test Base. While not well known, the site played a critical role in the United States' triumph in World War Two. The U.S. Navy's first use of the Salton Sea was in the Date Palm Beach area in the northeast corner, where it practiced training for bombing target practice and emergency procedures with seaplanes. At the onset of World War Two, the Navy expanded its operations at the sea and acquired 3,520 acres at its current site. The base was commissioned as the Salton Sea Naval Auxiliary Air Station in the fall of 1942. Designed for operational training for naval fleet units, the base supported twelve twin-engined PBY Catalina seaplanes. By 1944, the station was upgraded to accommodate air-to-ground rocket training, and an airfield with two 4,000-foot clay runways was built just inland from the seaplane base. Barracks and support for over 600 men were also constructed.

Meanwhile, the Salton Sea Base was being utilized for a pivotal top-secret role in ending the war. Lt.-Col. Paul Tibbets led the 509th Composite Group from the Wendover Army Air Base in Utah to secretly practice atomic bombing runs. Before dropping the first atomic bomb on Hiroshima, Tibbets and his crews made over 150 practice runs with dummy atom bombs. Taking off in Utah, the B-29s would fly to the Salton Sea and drop their prototype bombs from 30,000 feet, aiming at wooden targets built on pilings in the water near the base. Perfecting the delicate maneuvers after the bomb drop to evade the nuclear blast was also critical.

After the war, the naval base was decommissioned and the facility was turned over to Sandia National Labs as a contractor for the Atomic Energy Commission. The site was used for testing Nike missiles, drone airplanes, and other weapons systems. Some of the tests used depleted uranium.

By 1967, the base was taken over by the Naval Air Facility El Centro, which used the location sparingly until 1979. While the Navy conducted testing for parachute systems for manned space flights and other military testing during that period, the constant problem of severely fluctuating water levels of the Salton Sea made the facility hard to utilize. By 1986, the base was largely abandoned and most of its buildings destroyed. The site's final hurrah was for training and live-fire practice for Marines and Navy Seals during the Gulf War conflict.

Decommissioned since the mid-1990s, it has become a hard spot to visit as the base is nearly inaccessible by car. An attempt to drive to the base location directly from CA Route 86 is met with a 25-foot wall of sand blocking the way. Giant, shifting sand dunes have completely overtaken the roads directly leading to the complex. Due to the declining water levels at the sea, it is now possible to visit the ruins via high-ground clearance four-wheel-drive vehicles from an approach from the south and up the coast. The crumbling base has a bizarre collection of forsaken structures and leftover debris. The first thing that one notices at the base site is the pilings of the massive boat and seaplane dock which used to jut into the Salton Sea. It hints at the original height of the water level and the position of the now receded shoreline. The few remaining buildings are peppered with bullet holes; it is unclear whether they were shot up by vandals, servicemen in training, or both.

The Road to the Base. Salton Sea Naval Base. 2016

Embedded F150 Truck. Salton Sea Naval Base. 2016

Unexploded Ordnance Warning Sign,
Salton Sea Naval Base. 2014

Unexploded Ordnance Warning Sign,
Salton Sea Naval Base. 2019

Dock Corner. Salton Sea Naval Base. 2019

Dock Pilings. Salton Sea Naval Base. 2019

Tire Bumper. Salton Sea Naval Base. 2019

Oily Shore. Salton Sea Naval Base. 2019

Crucifix. Salton Sea Naval Base. 2019

Disintegrated Car. Salton Sea Naval Test Base. 2019

Building T. Salton Sea Naval Test Base. 2019

Electrical Panel, Building T. Salton Sea Naval Test Base. 2019

Window, Building T. Salton Sea Naval Test Base. 2019

Downed Electrical Pole. Salton Sea Naval Test Base. 2019

Building A-1. Salton Sea Naval Test Base. 2019

Upper Deck, Building A-1. Salton Sea Naval Test Base. 2019

Askania Ballistic Camera Pedestal, Building A-1. Salton Sea Naval Test Base. 2019

Matching Set. Salton Sea Naval Base. 2019

9

SALTON CITY

By the late 1950s, the Salton Sea had become one of California's prime tourist destinations, at times with even more visitors than Yosemite National Park. To take advantage of the popularity, real estate mogul M. Penn Phillips aggressively marketed a planned community on the western shore called Salton City. Sold as "The West's Greatest Playground," Phillips and his company designed a 19,600-acre subdivision. They created the infrastructure to support a street grid with 250 miles of paved roads, with full electrical, water, and sewer services. Plans for an airport, schools, churches, parks, swimming pools, and an eighteen-hole PGA golf course were drafted. A gorgeous Albert Frey- designed seaside resort called the Salton Bay Yacht Club was constructed, becoming an icon of the Salton City development.

When Salton City was opened to investors in 1958, investors lined up in droves to own a piece of the "Salton Riviera," which seemed at the time to be an unmissable investment. There were $4.25 million of lot sales that year. Between 1958 and 1964, 32,000 residential lots were sold, and over $20 million was spent developing the town.

Most of those lots proved to have been purchased for investment purposes only, as relatively few homes were ever built on them. As such, the town has long had an exceptionally eerie quality, with miles and miles of paved roads with street signs with names like "Sea Manor Avenue," but almost no homes. The same issues that plagued the rest of the Salton Sea in the 1970s—higher water salinity, overwhelming odor, flooding, algae blooms, and fish death—hurt Salton City, too.

The town was host to the Salton City 500-Mile Championship Boat Race, which ran a triangle-shaped 2.5-mile course. Due to the optimal conditions in Salton City, with plenty of space on the shore for racing teams to set up pits, the race became one of the most important and prominent events in the sport. Some 200 hot-rodded speedboats would compete in each race, traveling at speeds up to 80 miles an hour.

25,000 spectators came to view the first yearly event in 1961, with subsequent races drawing over 60,000 people. Celebrity racers, such as actor Lon Chaney, Jr., and astronaut Gordon Cooper, helped make the race even more popular. After successfully running the race for ten years, the Salton City 500 was permanently canceled after flooding decimated the town's coastal infrastructure.

Presently, the shoreline has now greatly receded away from town and the marina, and the yacht club and its hotel have been totally demolished. The golf course has long been closed and the areas near the coast seem largely abandoned. Surprisingly, the town's population has grown to about 5,000 residents in recent years, up from about 1,000 in the year 2000. Most of the new residents have settled in the westernmost part of town, away from the coastline and closer to CA Route 86. That area is closer to a newer casino development on Native American lands to the northwest, and farther from the ubiquitous "Salton Sea Stench" on the shore. The repopulation of Salton City sets a hopeful tone for the revitalization of the Salton Sea.

Palms Trees, Salton Bay Yacht Club. Salton City. 2014

Portal. Salton City. 2017

Red Trailer, Salton City. 2015

Red Trailer, Salton City. 2017

Trailer Interior. Salton City. 2013

Boat in Front Yard. Salton City. 2019

Tilapia Nests. Salton City. 2019

Fish Carcass. Salton City. 2016

Cabaña Row. Salton City. 2019

Cabaña Window. Salton City. 2017

Old Friends. Salton City. 2015

The Very End. Salton City. 2019

BIBLIOGRAPHY

Books

Blake, K., *Salton Sea Resort: Death in the Desert* (Minneapolis, MN, Bearport Publishing Co., 2015)
Pepper, C., *Desert Lore of Southern California* (El Cajon, CA, Sunbelt Publications, 1999)
Stringfellow, K., *Greetings From The Salton Sea: Folly and Intervention in the Southern California Landscape, 1905-2005* (Chicago, IL, The Center for American Places, Inc., 2005)
Trover, E. L., *Birth of the Inland Sea: How the Colorado River Created The Salton Sea, 1905-2005* (Coachella, CA, History Trove Publication, 2018)

Maps

Kym's Guide, *Map of Salton Sea* No. 1, 1:155,000 (Triumph Press Inc., Glendale, CA., 1961).

Films

SOS: The Salton Sea Walk. Dir. Corbin Schweitzer. Black Moon Prods. 2017. Amazon Prime Video.

Websites (all last retrieved on December 17, 2019)

airfields-freeman.com/CA/Airfields_CA_SanBernardino_NE.htm
asprs.org/wp-content/uploads/pers/1961journal/mar/1961_mar_51-55.pdf
atlasobscura.com/places/bombay-beach
boatracingfacts.com/forums/showthread.php?17156-Salton-Sea-Speedboats-in-the-Desert
cdnc.ucr.edu/?a=d&d=SBS19571128.1.10&e=-------en--20--1--txt-txIN--------1
cdnc.ucr.edu/cgi-bin/cdnc?a=d&d=DS19641103.2.75&e=-------en--20--1--txt-txIN--------1
censusreporter.org/profiles/16000US0619024-desert-shores-ca/
content.cdlib.org/view?docId=kt8p30069f;NAAN=13030&chunk.id=d0e6801&toc.id=&toc.depth=1&brand=calisphere&anchor.id=tab2
desertsun.com/story/opinion/editorials/2019/11/01/imperial-county-emergency-declaration-must-renew-salton-sea-urgency-desert-sun-editorial-board/4127780002
en.wikipedia.org/wiki/Eagle_Mountain_Railroad
en.wikipedia.org/wiki/North_Shore_Beach_and_Yacht_Club

en.wikipedia.org/wiki/Salton_Buttes
en.wikipedia.org/wiki/Slab_City,_California
en.wikisource.org/wiki/Popular_Science_Monthly/Volume_70/January_1907/The_Possibilities_of_Salton_Sea
escholarship.org/content/qt3jv444hn/qt3jv444hn.pdf?t=pxewk7
facebook.com/EcoMediaCompass/posts/sosyesterday-i-drove-out-to-speak-with-the-owner-of-the-property-old-man-leo-bor/545527625535942/
facebook.com/groups/64337476896/permalink/10157332877786897
facebook.com/scweatherforce/photos/a.1581105165496933/2369576799983095
greetingsfromsaltonsea.com/military.html
historytrove.com/2019/02/19/new-liverpool-salt-works/
lao.ca.gov/Publications/Report/3879
latimes.com/archives/la-xpm-1999-aug-12-mn-65092-story.html
latimes.com/environment/story/2019-12-09/a-new-dilemma-in-the-salton-sea-saga-unintended-marshlands
legendsofamerica.com/ca-saltonsea/
lostamerica.com/photo-items/the-salton-sea/
maps.roadtrippers.com/us/salton-city-ca/attractions/abandoned-salton-riviera
militarymuseum.org/NAASSaltonSea.html
phys.org/news/2015-03-salton-sea-time-bomb-california-drought.html
reddit.com/r/CoachellaValley/comments/2wqfxq/history_of_bank_building_in_niland/
saltonseawalk.com/the-salton-seas-sunken-city/
sandiegouniontribune.com/sdut-history-of-the-salton-sea-2015jun02-story.html
science.howstuffworks.com/environmental/conservation/issues/salton-sea.htm
theculturetrip.com/north-america/usa/california/articles/everything-you-need-to-know-about-californias-slab-city/
theverge.com/2018/6/6/17433294/salton-sea-crisis-drying-up-asthma-toxic-dust-pictures
waterdata.usgs.gov/nwis/dv?referred_module=sw&cb_62614=on
worldofindie.co.uk/?p=773
www2.calstate.edu/impact-of-the-csu/research/wrpi/Documents/conference/2018/Panel-1-2Burks.pdf

ABOUT THE AUTHOR

ANDY WILLINGER is an artist, photographer, writer, and creative originally from New York City. As the son of a Madison Avenue creative director and the stepson of a photojournalist, he was raised to appreciate the importance of striking visuals and clever storytelling. Willinger studied at Boston University, earning a B.S. Degree in broadcasting and film. He came to California in 1990, where he fell in love with the capacious horizons of the desert and the sea, living in both Los Angeles and the Joshua Tree area. After establishing a successful career in television, Andy continues to be a devoted explorer of the delicate beauty and unforgiving desolation of the American Southwest. His photographs are collected and displayed worldwide.